The Marvelous Arithmetics of Distance

OTHER BOOKS BY AUDRE LORDE

The Marvelous Arithmetics of Distance

P O E M S   1 9 8 7   -   1 9 9 2

Audre Lorde

W · W · Norton & Company   *New York*   *London*

Some of these poems were originally published in
Callaloo, The Caribbean Writer, MS Magazine, Nimrod, and *Quack Magazine.*

The text of this book is composed in Garamond #3,
with the display set in Belwe.
Composition by PennSet, Inc.
Manufacturing by The Courier Companies, Inc.
Book design by Guenet Abraham.

Library of Congress Cataloging-in-Publication Data

Lorde, Audre.
The marvelous arithmetics of distance / Audre Lorde.
p.   cm.
I. Title.
PS3562.075M37   1993
811'.54—dc20   92-40859

ISBN 0-393-03513-1

W. W. Norton & Company, Inc., 500 Fifth Avenue, New York, NY 10110

W. W. Norton & Company Ltd., 10 Coptic Street, London WC1A 1PU

1 2 3 4 5 6 7 8 9 0

To My Sister Pat Parker, Poet and
Comrade-in-Arms In Memoriam

and to my blood sisters
Mavis Jones
Marjorie Jones
Phyllis Blackwell
Helen Lorde

CONTENTS

The Marvelous
Arithmetics
of Distance

SMELLING THE WIND

Rushing headlong
into new silence
your face
dips on my horizon
the name
of a cherished dream
riding my anchor
one sweet season
to cast off
on another voyage

No reckoning allowed
save the marvelous arithmetics
of distance

LEGACY—HERS

When love leaps from my mouth
cadenced in that Grenada wisdom
upon which I first made holy war
then I must reassess
all my mother's words
or every path I cherish.

Like everything else I learned from Linda
this message hurtles across still uncalm air
silent   tumultuous   freed water
descending an imperfect drain.

I learn how to die
from your many examples
cracking the code of your living
heroisms   collusions   invisibilities
constructing my own
book of your last hours
how we tried to connect
in that bland spotless room
one bright Black woman
to another   bred for endurance
for battle

>   *island women make good wives*
>   *whatever happens they've seen worse . . .*

your last word to me was   *wonderful*
and I am still seeking the rest
of that terrible acrostic

MAKING LOVE TO CONCRETE

An upright abutment in the mouth
of the Willis Avenue bridge
a beige Honda leaps the divider
like a steel gazelle   inescapable
sleek leather boots on the pavement
rat-a-tat-tat   best intentions
going down for the third time
stuck   in the particular

You cannot make love to concrete
if you care about being
non-essential   wrong or worn   thin
if you fear ever becoming
diamonds or lard
you cannot make love to concrete
if you cannot pretend
concrete needs your loving

To make love to concrete
you need an indelible feather
white dresses before you are ten
a confirmation lace veil   milk-large bones
and aid raid drills in your nightmares
no stars till you go to the country
and one summer when you are twelve
Con Edison pulls the plug
on the street-corner moons   Walpurgisnacht
and there are sudden new lights in the sky
stone chips that forget   you need

to become a light rope   a hammer
a repeatable bridge
garden-fresh broccoli   two dozen dropped eggs
and a hint of you
caught up between my fingers
the lesson of a wooden beam
propped up on barrels
across the mined terrain

between forgiving too easily
and never giving at all.

ECHOES

There is a timbre of voice
that comes from not being heard
and knowing   you are not being
heard   noticed only
by others   not heard
for the same reason.

The flavor of midnight fruit   tongue
calling your body through dark light
piercing the allure of safety
ripping the glitter of silence
around you
          dazzle me with color
          and perhaps I won't notice
till after you're gone
your hot grain smell tattooed
into each new poem   resonant
beyond escape   I am listening
in that fine space
between desire and always
the grave stillness
before choice.

As my tongue unravels
in what pitch
will the scream hang unsung
or shiver like lace on the borders
of never   recording

which dreams heal   which
dream can kill
stabbing a man and burning his body
for cover   being caught
making love to a woman
I do not know.

DOMINO

On Thursday she buried her featherbed
at the foot of the garden
a Manx cat's bleached pelvic bone
twirled in the sun.

She had never intended to stay
so long   horizons burning
past forsythia   bracken
all roads out of her dooryard
folded in
upon reflection.

Every full moon
the neighborhood cats
came to worship
to wait   in a grim line
under the apple tree
the cat-bone swings
to a heavy beat

Sharpeville
Amritsar
Shatila
Birmingham Sunday

Imagine yourself
alabama
wanting to weep.

THAW

The language of past seasons
collapses   pumpkins in spring
false labor slides like mud
off the face of ease
and whatever I turn my hand to
pales in the sun.

We will always be there to your call
the old witches said
always said   always saying
something else   at the same time
you are trapped   asleep
you are speechless
perhaps   you will also be
broken.

Step lightly   all around us
words are cracking
off   we drift
separate and syllabic
if we survive at all.

PARTY TIME

Newspapers printed in secret report
bent needles under the child's fingernail
barbed stitches through the bleeding scalp
grandchildren playing hide and seek
riddled with bullets behind a silk-cotton tree
just two more funerals in Soweto
behind the small coffins
Lillian's son-in-law drags his feet
achilles tendons shredded by police dogs
festering   in their eyes
each memory of home
poised over potshards in the dawn.*

But who sings the song
of my mothers' muscled beauty
these large sore-bodied women
with nimble tongues   gnarled ankles
stepping to an elegant rhythm
arms akimbo in quick march time
rocking with laughter   and the young ones
strut   without illusion
weathered extreme bodies

---

* Potshards left on a woman's hearthstone are a sign one of her sons
did not survive an initiation rite.

blossom   in the singing night
Lillian's hooded eyes invite me
into the circle   a strum of voices
weaving an intricate drum.

Over grapejuice in South Provence
the women from South Africa
lower their voices   discussing rents
and who has not yet paid   a protest
punishable by death
burning through the Mofolo night.

Eleanor Bumpurs, grandmother,
shotgunned
against her kitchen wall
by rent marshals in the Bronx
moves among us   humming
her breath is sweet acacia
in this stone yard at sunset
rhythms quicken
and I come next   behind her
in our dance.

Prism

For Joyce Serote

There are no frogs in Soweto
students croak
Amandla! through the tear-gas.

Not true no frogs live in Soweto
only we are too weary
with no ears left to hear them.

Who knows where frogs live in Soweto
who has time to listen
stroll along a moonlit gutter
beyond the flames of evening
rising   falling
the thin high screams
of skewered children.

In the bruising fist of challenge
the future does not tarry.

Take our words to bed with you
dream upon them
choose any ones you wish
write us a poem.

DO YOU REMEMBER LAURA

Alive
between the Panther News and Zabar's
an Upper West Side proper
exiled to Brooklyn
where she became a style
Broadway in the winter and the rain
long fingers flashing
Red Zinger tea at Teacher's
next to Bolton's
piperack elegance.

One unguarded turn
from curb to never
the car leaps my control
like an adolescent girl
one hand against the windshield
in surprise   another
saying no   I did not choose this
death   I want my say.

Forgive me Laura
I could have been your lover
in time longing skids   crashes
but does not self-destruct.

INHERITANCE—HIS

I.

My face resembles your face
less and less each day. When I was young
no one mistook whose child I was.
Features   build   coloring
alone among my creamy fine-boned sisters
marked me Byron's daughter.

No sun set when you died, but a door
opened onto my mother. After you left
she grieved her crumpled world aloft
an iron fist sweated with business symbols
a printed blotter   *dwell in a house of Lord's*
your hollow voice chanting down a hospital corridor
              yea, though I walk through the valley
              of the shadow of death
              I will fear no evil.

II.

I rummage through the deaths you lived
swaying on a bridge of question.
At seven   in Barbados
dropped into your unknown father's life
your courage vault from his tailor's table
back to the sea
Did the Grenada treeferns sing
your 15th summer as you jumped ship

to seek your mother
finding her   too late
surrounded with new sons?

Who did you bury to become enforcer of the law
the handsome legend
before whose raised arm even trees wept
a man of deep and wordless passion
who wanted sons and got five girls?
You left the first two scratching in a treefern's shade
the youngest is a renegade poet
searching for your answer in my blood.

My mother's Grenville tales
spin through early summer evenings.
But you refused to speak of home
of stepping proud Black and penniless
into this land where only white men
ruled by money.   How you labored
in the docks of the Hotel Astor
your bright wife a chambermaid upstairs
welded love and survival to ambition
as the land of promise withered
crashed   the hotel closed
and you peddle dawn-bought apples
from a pushcart on Broadway.
Does an image of return
wealthy and triumphant

warm your chilblained fingers
as you count coins in the Manhattan snow
or is it only Linda
who dreams of home?

When my mother's first-born crys for milk
in the brutal city winter
do the faces of your other daughters dim
like the image of the treeferned yard
where a dark girl first cooked for you
and her ash heap still smells curry?

III.

Did the secret of my sisters steal your tongue
like I stole money from your midnight pockets
stubborn and quaking
as you threaten to shoot me if I am the one?
the naked lightbulbs in our kitchen ceiling
glint off your service revolver
as you load   whispering.

Did two little dark girls in Grenada
dart like flying fish
between your averted eyes
and my pajamaless body
our last adolescent summer
eavesdropped orations

to your shaving mirror
our most intense conversations
were you practicing how to tell me
of my twin sisters   abandoned
as you had been abandoned
by another Black woman seeking
her fortune   Grenada   Barbados
Panama   Grenada.
New York City.

IV.

You bought old books at auction
for my unlanguaged world
gave me your idols   Marcus Garvey   Citizen Kane
and morsels from your dinner plate
when I was seven.
I owe you my Dahomeyan jaw
the free high school for gifted girls
no one else thought I should attend
and the darkness that we share.
Our deepest bonds remain
the mirror and the gun.

V.

An elderly Black judge
known for his way with women

visits this island where I live
shakes my hand, smiling
"I knew your father," he says
"quite a man!" Smiles again.
I flinch at his raised eyebrow.
A long-gone woman's voice
lashes out at me   in parting
"You will never be satisfied
until you have the whole world
in your bed!"

Now I am older than you were when you died
overwork and silence exploding in your brain.
You are gradually receding from my face.
Who were you outside the 23rd Psalm?
Knowing so little
how did I become so much
like you?

Your hunger for rectitude
blossoms into rage
the hot tears of mourning
never shed for you before
your twisted measurements
the agony of denial
the power of unshared secrets.

January 23–September 10, 1992

The One Who Got Away

The youngest sister
works a dangerous ground
mildewed   combustible
beyond glamour or choice
she is last seen
leaping the dangerous pegmatite
under noon's mercy.

Each day she lives
a bright ransom
going away   beyond the guilty
cut to the border   evening
hounds baying across the clearing.

Each day a new landscape
but never a woman
peeks out from the folds
of her bed-scented mirror
to whisper   you are the fairest
daughter.

And every midnight
over her nightmare's shoulder
a swollen girl
belly pressed against glass
waves goodbye
through the slanting rain.

DEPRECIATION

Staten Island, 1986

First the plumbing breaks down
a minor valve slips with a hiss
as the first guests sit down
amontillado in hand.

Between the leek soup and curried flounder
an era begins in the basement
the furnace gives up
its castiron forevers   slowly
the pump stutters   groans
refusing to move
we promise each other
future celebrations.

SYRACUSE AIRPORT

Clean jeans and comfortable shoes
I need no secrets here   at home
in this echoless light
I spread my papers out
around me.

Opposite   alert
a grey-eyed lady takes fire
one pale nostril quivering
we both know women
who take up space
are called sloppy.

Thanks to Jesse Jackson

January 1, 1989

The US and the USSR
are/were the most powerful countries
in the world
but only ⅛ of the world's population.
African people are also ⅛ of the world's population.
½ of the world's people are Asian.
½ of that number is Chinese.

There are 22 nations in the Middle East.

So most people in this world
are Yellow, Black, Brown, Poor, Female
Non-Christian
and do not speak english.

By the year 2000
the 20 largest cities in the world
will have two things in common
none of them will be in Europe
and none in the United States.

JUDITH'S FANCY

Half-built
your greathouse looms
between me and the sun.
Shell-smells on the morning wind.
You are younger than my daughter
the boy you hold is blond
the moon is new.
My sloping land brings our eyes level
"Welcome, neighbor," I begin.

Were we enemies in another life
or do your eyes always turn to flint
when meeting a Black woman
face to face?

Your child speaks first.
"I don't like you," he cries
"Are you coming to babysit me?"

PRODUCTION

100,000 bees make a sturdy hive
ready   three days after the moon is full
we cut honey.

Our hot knives slice the caps of wax
from each heavy frame
dark pollened richness drips
from the laden combs.

Sadiq loads the extractor
Curtis leveling the spin.
Sweet creeps like bees
through each crack of hot air.

Outside the honey house
hungry drones cluster
low-voiced and steady
we strain the flow   laughing
drunk with honey.

Before twilight
long rows of bottles stand
labeled and waiting.

Tomorrow we make a living
two dollars at a time.

BUILDING

Gloria has a permit
to change the earth
plucks flies
from the air
while discussing
revolution
is taken for local
in a lot
of different places.

JESSEHELMS

I am a Black woman
writing my way to the future
off a garbage scow knit from moral fiber
stuck together with jessehelms'
come   where Art is a dirty word
scrawled on the wall
of Bilbo's memorial outhouse
and obscenity is catching
even I'd like to hear you scream
ream out your pussy
with my dildo called Nicaragua
ram Grenada up your fighole
till Panama runs out of you
like Savimbi aflame.

But you prefer to do it
on the senate floor
amid a sackful of paper pricks
keeping time to a 195 million dollar
military band
safe-sex dripping from your tongue
into avid senatorial ears.

Later you'll get yours
behind the senate toilets
where they're waiting for you jessehelms
those white boys with their pendulous rules
bumping against the rear door of Europe

spread-eagled across the globe
their crystal balls poised over Africa
ass-up for old glory.

Your turn now jessehelms
come on its time
to lick the handwriting
off the walls.

DEAR JOE

if you have ever tried to reach me
and I could not hear you
these words are in place of the dead air
still between us.
  —"Morning Is a Time for Miracles"

How many other dark young men at 33
left their public life   becoming legend
the mysterious connection
between whom we murder
and whom we mourn?

Everyone here likes our blossoms
permanent
and the flowers around your casket
will never die
preserved without error
in the crystals between our lashes
they will never bang down the phone
in our jangled ears at 3:30 AM
nor call us to account for our silence
nor refuse to answer
or say get away from me
this is my way   or say
we are wrong   prejudiced   lazy
deluded   cowardly   insignificant   faint
or say fuck you seven times in one sentence
when the circumstance of our lives
becomes so chaotic
words fly away like drunken buzzards

or say we might fail   or say
we might fail but that's no reason
to stop   to miss a beat
and the tinny jukebox music
comes up through the floor of our shoes.

Nobody here will lean too heavily
on your flowers
nor lick the petals of the lavender gladiola
for a hint of sweetness
wilting it with a whiskey blast
threatening the faint-hearted
with a handshake or a bottle of beer.

In the side pews   always ghosts
who resemble
our brothers   past and future
who say they were also our lovers   but they lie
terror caught in their throats like a lump of clay
and the taxi is waiting to take them back
out to the sunshine.

A pale refugee from a nameless country
hawks wired roses from stool to stool
down the street
at the Pathmark Pharmacy
a drag-queen with burgundy long-johns
and a dental dam in his mouth
is buying a straight razor.

WOMEN ON TRAINS

For Jacqui and Angela

Leaving the known for another city
the club-car smells of old velvet
rails whisper relief mantras
steel upon steel
every fourth thud breaks the hum
"stand and fight," I said
leaving my words for ransom
"your only way out."

This train is a doorway
bent into the shape of a scale.

Eleanor Roosevelt riding the rails
behind her husband's casket
forefinger tense along a propped cheek
one knuckle caressing her lips
young Nell's dreams strung along
sentinel stalks of mullein
giving
in the whip of the journey's wind
my mother's mandatory hat
at a no-nonsense tilt
beside the tenement windows of wartime
scanning Lenox Avenue
for a coal-delivery truck.

Women on trains
have a life

that is exactly livable
the precision of days flashing past
no intervention allowed
and the shape of each season
relentlessly carved in the land.

I have soared over crannied earth
spread like a woman waiting
but this angled sky anchors me
inward   through the ugliness
shards of bright fireweed   loosestrife
and stacks of heat-treated lumber   beyond
the bare arms of scrub-maple and poplar
already ablush.

Was it ever business as usual for these women
as snow-driven hopes and fears swirled
past tenement office windows
and nappy-topped stands of unreachable trees
flowed along in the southern dusk?

The coal truck arrived after dark   dumping
barely half-a-ton of bituminous
my father gone to his second job
she shoveled it down herself
in the freezing Harlem night
and coal dusted my mother's tired hat
as the subway screamed us home.

Women on trains have a chance
to unweave their tangles.
Perhaps between Blythe and Patchoula
Eleanor chose to live her own days.
The subway tunnel walls
closed in like thunder
and my mother never had a chance
to lay her magic down.

Between new lumber and the maples
I rehear your question
owning
the woman who breaks   the woman
who is broken.

I counseled you unwisely my sister
to be who I am   no longer
willing to be for my living
stopgap   hurled into the breach
beyond support   beyond change
and I search these rushing sun-dark trees
for your phone number
to acknowledge
both you and I
are free to go.

The Politics of Addiction

17 luxury condominiums
electronically protected
from criminal hunger   the homeless
seeking a night's warmth
across from the soup kitchen
St. Vincent's Hospital
razor wire covering the hot air grates.
Disrobed need
shrieks through the nearby streets.

Some no longer beg.
a brown sloe-eyed boy
picks blotches from his face
eyes my purse shivering
white dust a holy fire
in his blood
at the corner   fantasy
parodies desire   replaces longing
Green light.   The boy turns back
to the steaming grates.

Down the street in a show-window
camera   Havana
the well-shaped woman smiles
waves her plump arm along
half-filled market shelves
excess expectation
dusts across her words

"Si hubieran capitalismo
hubiesen tomates aquí!"
"If we had capitalism
tomatoes would be here now."

KITCHEN LINOLEUM

The cockroach
who is dying
and the woman
who is blind
agree
not to notice
each other's shame.

OSHUN'S TABLE

Amsterdam, 1986

How the fruit lay at your feet
how you dressed the wine
cut green beans
in a lacy network
wound to the drum
russet arm hairs
in the candlelight
we ate pom and fish rice
with a fork and spoon.

A short hard rain
and the moon came up
before we lay down together
we toasted each other
descendants of poets
and woodcutters
handsome
untrustworthy
and brave.

PARTING

I talk to rocks
sometimes they answer
double-voiced
as a woman in love
taking leave
in roars of jade.

Carnelian promises an end to bleak
through secret eyes of malachite
I look toward obsidian
to absolve my dreaming.

The jasper-red stone
in the gizzard of swallows
heals the moon-touched
the poor   and the disagreeable.

But it refuses to be taken
leaps off the sideboard
out of my loving fingers
hurls itself from the prow
of a borrowed canoe

And the swirling adventurine water
chants a coral   carved
with your moon-rock's name.

PEACE ON EARTH

Christmas, 1989

A six-pointed star
in the eyes of a Polish child
lighting her first shabbas candle   fading
into a painted cross on the Berlin Wall
gnarled Lithuanian hands at prayer
Romania's solemn triumph
a dictator's statue ground into dust
(SINTI-What?)*

Before the flickering screen
goes dead   rows of erupting houses
the rockets' red glare   where
are all these brown children
running scrambling around the globe
flames through the rubble
bombs bursting in air
Panama   Nablus   Gaza
tear gas clouding the Natal sun.

THIS IS A GIFT FROM THE PEOPLE
OF THE UNITED STATES OF AMERICA†
quick cut
the crackling Yule Log
in an iron grate.

---

* Sinti-Roma: the correct name for the still oppressed so-called Gypsy
   people of Romania.
† Stamped in large print on all emergency food packages sent to con-
   quered countries.

RESTORATION: A MEMORIAL—9/18/91

Berlin again   after chemotherapy
I reach behind me once more
for days to come
sweeping around the edges of authenticity
two years after Hugo blew one life away
Death like a burnt star
perched on the rim of my teacup
flaming the honey drips from my spoon
sunlight flouncing off the gargoyles opposite.

Somewhere it is Tuesday
in the ordinary world
ravishment fades
into compelling tasks
our bodies learn to perform
quite a bit of the house is left
our bedroom spared
except for the ankle-deep water
and terrible stench.

Would I exchange this safety of exile
for the muddy hand-drawn water
wash buckets stashed
where our front porch had been
half-rotten vegetables
the antique grey settling over your face
that October?

I want you laughing again
After the stinking rugs are dragged away
the crystal chandelier dug
from the dining-room floor
refrigerator righted
broken cupboards stacked outside
to dry for our dinner fire.

A few trees still stand
in a brand-new landscape
but the sea road is impassable.
Your red shirt
hung out on a bush to dry
is the only flower for weeks.
No escape. No return.
No other life
half so sane.

In this alien and temporary haven
my poisoned fingers
slowly return to normal
I read your letter dreaming
the perspective of a bluefish
or a fugitive parrot
watch the chemicals leaving my nails
as my skin takes back its weaknesses.
Learning to laugh again.

STARTING ALL OVER AGAIN

January 1, 1992

It's great to be able to call you
at strange hours of my night
asking you to explain
yourself   wondering
if that land you approach
radar in hand
climbing an unknown sea
where sailors dare not go lightly
is my face   your grandfather's
broad-lipped island face
so like mine
is your own face.

It is not wrong to hunger
for a cause   till the need
burns upriver
to your heart   becomes
an unquenchable taste
only you must believe
yourself
and the power to choose
your own selves
your best campaign.

I believe in you my son
and I tremble
but the whole earth is trembling
and no one is talking

more than 100,000 dead bodies
in the strange land between us
and still no word spoken
but you share my sleep
with a Kuwaiti girl
impaled twice
by the sprouting hatred of a conqueror
whose face is hidden from me
and by her brother
who loathes the child she bears.

Dark incandescent winds blow
the belch of smoldering oil wells
around the world
dimming my island sunsets
mingling with the black smoke
of Ellen Goodman's son
aflame on the Amherst green.

In one month I celebrate
the beginning of my second Saturn return
you were the gift of my first
and I trust you   beyond question

In what do you believe?

WHAT IT MEANS TO BE BEAUTIFUL

The child believes
what she sees
becomes her own
each morning   over toothpaste
in front of the mirror
another woman's mouth
goes tight as a zipper.

On the night wall
desire hangs
Virgin   unattainable
a tiny white woman smiling
the perfect fantasy of my sister
chains the door she opens
to wave me goodbye
admitting no common air
no debt to our morning.

I stumble over her threshold
razor wire   under the clothesline
I am scolded for inattention
lick where the iron flavor wells
hide   an unbitten star-apple
melting to sludge in my palm.

HUGO I

A coral stone at the edge of Bufano Road
where the storm sat down
but did not sleep
the jack pine I used to curse
for its ragged outline
as the evening shadows walked
across yucca stumps
where quits perched all last summer
fussing their yellow song.

A grey dog lay in the road
pregnant with death
as I planted new bougainvillea
that fortnight Gloria went North.

This skeleton was an almond tree.
That stalk a prickly pear cactus
green as a gourd
a peep of red fruit
promised and warned
in the same sticky breath.

All the rest is rubble.
Constructions
that fester and grow loathsome

because they cannot self-destruct.
In some fantasy of immortality
a wilted wisdom formed them
to last 10,000 years.

But the wind is our teacher.

CONSTRUCTION

Timber seasons better
if it is cut in the fourth quarter
of a barren sign.

In Cancer
the most fertile of skysigns
I shall build a house
that will stand forever.

SPEECHLESS

At the foot of the steps a forest
strewn with breadcrumb fingers
sticky with loss
stuffed with seductive chaotic songs
like a goose bound for the oven
giddy trees wait   shaken.

In the wild arms of a twilit birch
the void of course moon
hangs like a spotlit breast.

Death
folds the corners of my mouth
into a heart-shaped star
sits on my tongue like a stone
around which your name blossoms
distorted.

FOR CRAIG

If I call you son and not brother
it is because I pray
my son learns your conceit   your daring
who came so late   and left too soon
If I call you brother and not son
it is to mourn my own loss
that my mother did not live long enough
to bear you.

You said we should always be brave
and I try to be   every morning
over my toothbrush and the waning stars
I peer through your eyes
through your taut heart's muscle
beating war rhythms
with determination
and a brush of bells.

EAST BERLIN

It feels dangerous now
to be Black in Berlin
sad suicides that never got reported
Neukölln   Kreuzberg   the neon Zoo
a new siege along Unter den Linden
with Paris accents   New York hustle
many tattered visions intersecting.

Already my blood shrieks
through East Berlin streets
misplaced hatreds
volcanic tallies rung upon cement
Afro-German woman stomped to death
by skinheads in Alexanderplatz
two-year-old girls
half-cooked in their campcots
who pays the price
for their disillusion?

Hand-held the candles wink
in Berlin's scant November light
hitting the Wall at 30 miles an hour
vision first
is still hitting a wall
and on the other side
the rank chasm

where dreams of laurels lie
hollowness wed to triumph
differing from defeat
only in the approaching tasks.

THE NIGHT-BLOOMING JASMINE

Lady of the Night   star-breathed
blooms along the searoad
between my house and the tasks before me
calls down a flute
carved from the legbone of a gull.

Through the core of me
a fine rigged wire
upon which pain will not falter
nor predict
I was no stranger to this arena
at high noon
beyond was not an enemy
to be avoided
but a challenge
against which my neck grew strong
against which my metal struck
and I rang like fire in the sun.

I still patrol that line
sword drawn
lighting red-glazed candles of petition
along the scar
the surest way of knowing
death is a fractured border
through the center of my days.

Bees seek their need
until flowers beckon
beyond the limit of their wings
then they drop where they fly
pollen baskets laden
the sweet work done.

They do not know the Lady of the Night
blossoms
between my house and the searoad
calling down a flute
carved from the legbone of a gull
your rich voice
riding the shadows of conquering air.

November 1990–May 1992

GIRLFRIEND
March 27, 1990

It's almost a year and I still
can't deal with you
not being
at the end of the line.

I read your name in memorial poems
and think they must be insane
mistaken   malicious
in terrible error
just plain wrong

not that there haven't been times before
months passing   madly   sadly
we not speaking
    get off my case, will you please?
    oh, just lighten up!

But I can't get you out
of my air   my spirit
my special hotline phone book
is this what it means to live
forever   when will I
not miss picking up the receiver
after a pregnancy of silence
one of us born again
with a brand-new address or poem
miffed
because the other doesn't jump
at the sound
of her beloved voice?

LUNAR ECLIPSE

August 16, 1989

Last night I watched the moon go out
become a dark opalescent glow
I could not believe what was happening
even as I saw the change in light.

The first time I met you
we sat up all night reading
each other's poems   morning hopes
followed us down Cole Street
chattering like a flock of quits.

You stretch across our best years
like a living wire
between heaven and hell
at war   Being sisters
wasn't always easy
but it was never dull.

I can't believe you are gone
out of my life
So you are not.

CHANGE

In whose bed
did I lie asweat
as the first thrush sounded
telling myself stories
of someone I used to be
hurling myself
at the unfamiliar shore
taunting the rocks' long shadow
till the waves beat my rage
back to spindrift
and my wars came home?

The girls who live
at the edge of the calm pool
where the moon rises
teach me
to leave dreams alone.

TODAY IS NOT THE DAY

I can't just sit here
staring death in her face
blinking and asking for a new name
by which to greet her

I am not afraid to say
unembellished
I am dying
but I do not want to do it
looking the other way.

Today is not the day.
It could be
but it is not.
Today is today
in the early moving morning
sun shining down upon
the farmhouse in my belly
lighting the wellswept alleys
of the town growing in my liver
intricate vessels swelling with the gift
of Mother Mawu
or her mischievous daughter
Afrekete   Afrekete   my beloved
feel the sun of my days surround you
binding our pathways
we have water to carry
honey to harvest

bright seed to plant for the next fair
we will linger
exchanging sweet oil
along each other's ashy legs
the evening light
a crest on your cheekbones.

By this rising
some piece of our labor
is already half-done
the taste of loving
doing a bit of work
having some fun
riding my wheels so close to the line
my eyelashes blaze.

Beth dangles her stethoscope over the rearview mirror
Jonathan fine-tunes his fix on Orion
working through another equation
youth taut as an arrow
stretched to their borders
the barb sinking in so far
it vanishes from the surface.
I dare not tremble for them
only pray laughter comes often enough
to soften the edge.

And Gloria   Gloria
whose difference I learn
with the love of a sister   you   you
in my eyes bright appetite   light
playing along your muscle
as you swing.

This could be the day.
I could slip anchor and wander
to the end of the jetty
uncoil into the waters
a vessel of light   moonglade
ride the freshets to sundown
and when I am gone
another stranger will find you
coiled on the warm sand
beached treasure   and love you
for the different stories
your seas tell
and half-finished blossoms
growing out of my season
trail behind
with a comforting hum.

But today
is not the day.
Today.

April 22, 1992

THE ELECTRIC SLIDE BOOGIE

New Year's Day 1:16 AM
and my body is weary beyond
time to withdraw and rest
ample room allowed me in everyone's head
but community calls
right over the threshold
drums beating through the walls
children playing their truck dramas
under the collapsible coatrack
in the narrow hallway outside my room

The TV lounge next door is wide open
it is midnight in Idaho
and the throb   easy   subtle   spin
of the electric slide boogie
step-stepping
around the corner of the parlor
past the sweet clink
of dining room glasses
and the edged aroma of slightly overdone
dutch-apple pie
all laced together
with the rich dark laughter
of Gloria
and her higher-octave sisters

How hard it is to sleep
in the middle of life.

January 3, 1992